AF417092

Darkness... Untold Tales (Collection of Fearful Happenings)

Anna Elizabeth

Copyright © [2024] by [Anna Elizabeth]

All rights reserved.

No portion of this book may be reproduced in any form without written permission from the publisher or author, except as permitted by U.S. copyright law.

Published by Jo Ann Gray

This is a work of fiction.

Contents

Darkness... Untold Tales

(Collection of Fearful Happenings)

Chapter 1

Ghost in the Mirror

The old mansion loomed at the end of Ravenwood Lanes, its once-grand facade now a patchwork of peeling paint and ivy. Its Victorian structure stood proudly, yet gloomy on the hilltop. Locals whispered about the place, sharing tales of the enigmatic figure that appeared in its windows at twilight. They said it was the spirit of Eleanor, the last of her long family lineage, who vanished mysteriously a century ago.

Lila, new to the town and armed with a curiosity that bordered on reckless, stood before the mansion's heavy oak door. It creaked open as if anticipating her arrival. She stepped inside, the air thick with ancient dust and the heavy scent of aged wood. Sunlight streamed through the broken panes, illuminating motes of dust that danced like tiny spirits through the air. Lila took a deep breath, sneezing from the floating motes, and whispered to herself as she pushed her dark curls of hair behind her ears, "It's just a story, just an old ghost tale this town likes to tell. I can do this; this is my new beginning, and I will make it work."

The hallway was lined with old portraits of stern-looking ancestors that belonged to the previous owner, their eyes seemingly following her every move. Lila felt a shiver run down her spine but shrugged it off quickly. She had always loved exploring forgotten, old places, old vintage homes, seeking out the hidden secrets they held. As she wandered deeper into the house, she found herself in what had once been the drawing room. The furniture lay draped in white sheets that had dust piled thick across them, as if frozen in time. A large, ornate mirror hung above the old fireplace; its surface tarnished but still slightly reflective.

Lila approached it, drawn by an inexplicable pull. As she peered into the glass, her reflection wavered, as she saw her brown eyes glistening in the dusty pane of the mirror, her messy long, brown hair stacked high on her head in a messy bun, and for a brief moment, she thought she saw a shadow flicker behind her. With her heart racing, she turned, but the room was empty, only herself dwelling within it. Just the quiet creaking of the old house settling.

"Get a grip, girl," Lila said to herself, forcing a nervous laugh, but when she turned back to the antique mirror, the flicker returned, this time much clearer, a mere figure in a flowing white and pink pastel dress, with dark hair cascading over her shoulders. Lila's breath caught in her throat.

"Eleanor?" she whispered fearfully, half expecting the figure to respond. Instead, it smiled faintly, a haunting expression that seemed both welcoming and sorrowful.

Before Lila could process what exactly it was that she was seeing, the mirror rippled, as if disturbed by a breeze. She reached out with a trembling hand instinctively, her fingers brushing against the cool surface of the mirror. Suddenly, the entire room darkened, shadows pooling in the corners, and the temperature dropped drastically.

"Help me..." a faint voice whispered, echoing in the silence.

Lila stepped back, her heart now pounding in her chest, her breathing at a steady pace. The reflection of the figure in the old mirror shifted, now filled with desperation. She wanted to run away in fear, but something just wouldn't allow her to do so, maybe, it was her dark curiosity that held her there.

"Help you?" she echoed in reply, her mind swirling with confusion.

The tales that she had heard since arriving in this town about Eleanor, weren't just mere ghost stories; they were real, a mere call for assistance. A chill swept through her, igniting a mix of fear and slight determination. With newfound resolve, Lila took a deep breath and sneezed again, as she leaned closer to the antique mirror, "What exactly do you want from me? What do you need, Eleanor?"

In that moment, the figure's eyes locked onto hers, filled with an urgency that sent a jolt of confused understanding through Lila. She wasn't just a spectator in this ghostly encounter; she was being pulled into a story that demanded to be truly unraveled. As the sunlight faded outside, casting eerie shadows across the room, Lila knew she had just crossed a forbidden threshold. The ghost in the mirror had awakened something within her, within her mere curiosity, a quest that could change everything she had ever known to be real. And somewhere deep inside, she felt the stirring of an adventure waiting to be unfolded.

As the lights flickered back on and the room became a warmer temperature, Lila stood there in amazement as the ghostly figure faded away.

Chapter 2

Collection of Fearful Happenings

The next morning, Lila awoke with the remnants of the previous day's events swirling in her mind like autumn leaves caught in a gust of wind. She rubbed her brown eyes, trying to shake off the feeling that something had shifted overnight. The sun streamed through her bedroom window, but the brightness did little to dispel the shadows of uncertainty that clung to her. Determined to uncover the mysterious truth behind the ghost, Eleanor, Lila grabbed her notebook and headed to the town library, unpacking all her boxes would have to wait. She hoped the dusty shelves might yield some type of clues about the mansion and its elusive occupant, maybe, some kind of history could be found that would help her understand.

The library was a cozy, quiet labyrinth, filled with the scent of old paper, old books, and the soft rustle of fragile pages being turned. Lila approached the librarian at her desk, an elderly woman with pointed glasses perched on the edge of her nose.

"Excuse me, do you have any information about the family of Eleanor? Any sort of family history?" Lila asked, her voice remaining steady despite her racing heart on the matter.

The librarian looked up, her brow furrowing, "Ah, the family of the ghost of Eleanor, such a tragic tale, indeed. They say the old mansion is haunted by her unrestful spirit... You're not planning to go there, are you?"

Lila nodded, undeterred, "I think I might have visited there already... you see I just purchased and moved into that old house..."

The librarian's expression turned grave, "Many have gone there, tried to live there, but few have ever returned or remained, none have ever left there with their mere wits intact. It's said that Eleanor vanished without a trace, and some even say she still roams the old halls, seeking revenge, or a release. You should be cautious in that creepy old house, my dear."

With that, the elderly lady led Lila to a section of the library filled with local history books and old newspaper clippings. Hours slipped by as Lila immersed herself in tales of the family of Eleanor; she discovered that they were wealthy, influential, yet shadowed by major misfortune. As Lila poured over the faded articles and documents, a pattern emerged; strange happenings had surrounded the family. Many mysterious fires, whispers in the night, and several sightings of dark, shadowy figures. The more Lila read, the more she felt the weight of the untold past pressing down on her. One particular article caught her attention, 'The Vanishing of Eleanor... A Mystery Unsolved'. It detailed her last known whereabouts... a grand ball that was held in the mansion's opulent ballroom. Guests reported seeing Eleanor dance alone, her eyes lost in a distant world. She was dressed to perfection with a lace dress that was white and pink pastel. When the old clock struck midnight, she was gone, disappeared, leaving only the scent of roses behind.

"Eleanor, what happened to you?" Lila whispered to the pages with much curiosity, feeling an inexplicable connection to the lost spirit.

That night, Lila decided to revisit the old room with the mirror. Armed with a flashlight, just in case everything goes dark again, and her notebook, she approached the looming structure, the door of the vacant room, as the moon rose high outside, casting eerie shadows across the grounds. Although, she turned every light in the old house on, she hesitated at the threshold, the air thick with almost tangible tension. Once inside, the familiar musty scent enveloped her, but this time, a sense of foreboding gripped her. The mere room itself felt different, charged with unnatural energy. Lila stepped cautiously toward the mirror, her heart beginning to pound in her chest.

"Show me," she urged, as she stood in front of the antique mirror, feeling both foolish and slightly brave, "Show me what happened, Eleanor?"

As if in response, the old mirror darkened, the surface swirling like a stormy sea. Images, faded, began to emerge in the glass, flickering candlelight, the vibrant silhouette of a ballroom filled with many elegantly dressed figures, and at the center was Eleanor, dancing with a partner whose face remained obscured. Lila leaned closer, captivated. Suddenly, the vision shifted. The faint ballroom was now empty, the hints of laughter replaced by an oppressive silence. Eleanor stood alone, her expression shifting from joy to confusion, then over swept by fear. A cold wind blew through the room, rattling the windowpanes and causing the shadows to stretch ominously.

"Help me," Eleanor's voice echoed in Lila's mind, piercing through the stillness of the room, "You must find the truth."

With a gasp, Lila stumbled back, her heart racing again. The air around her seemed to shimmer, and a chilling laugh echoed through the mansion, a sound both cruel and sorrowful. It was as if the house itself had awakened, reacting to her presence. As Lila turned to leave the room, the door slammed shut, trapping her inside. Panic surged through her entire being, and she franticly pressed her palms against the cold wood of the door, desperate to escape the room, but before she could react further, she caught a glimpse of movement in the mirror. Eleanor's reflection stared back at her, much clearer than before, her eyes wide with great urgency, "Find what was lost." Eleanor implored, her faint voice like a frantic whisper, "Before it's too late."

Then with a blinding flash of light, the vision shattered, leaving Lila gasping in the dark room. The air still felt electric, charged with a mixture of fear and energy, determination. She had stepped into a world of mysterious deceptions far beyond her mere understanding.

"Okay," Lila whispered nervously, still a little shaken, her voice trembling but resolute, "I will try to help you, Eleanor."

As the shadows seemed to still dance around her, the mere feeling that they were still there, Lila realized as she tried to ease her heavy breathing, that she was no longer just a curious girl exploring a haunting in her mansion. She was now a part of a real unsolved haunting, a collection of fearful happenings that had bound Eleanor's spirit to the mirror, to the old house, and Lila would do her best to unravel the threads of this mystery of the past, no matter the cost. She would be brave and find the truth of Eleanor's disappearance from so long ago.

Chapter 3

The Haunting of a Cat

Lila's heart raced slightly as she stood in her drawing room, the echo of Eleanor's desperate plea still ringing in her ears. The oppressive darkness felt alive, swirling with possibilities and threats alike. She took a deep breath, steeling herself for whatever lay ahead, but just as she turned to leave the room, a soft 'meow' broke the silence.

Startled, Lila scanned the room. A small, tabby cat emerged from the shadows, its green eyes glimmering like emeralds. It wove through the dust-covered furniture, its movements fluid and graceful. The black cat paused, fixing Lila with a curious gaze, as if assessing her presence. Its fur was shining like silk as the black hair shimmered in the pale lighting of the room.

"Hey there, little one," Lila said, kneeling down, "Where did you come from, what are you doing in here?"

The cat cautiously approached, brushing against her leg, leaving small fragments of black hair against her blue jeans. Lila couldn't help but smile. It was a small comfort amidst all the overwhelming atmosphere of the mansion, but something about the cat felt off... its gaze seemed to hold a depth of estranged understanding, almost like it had a story to tell. As she reached out to petit, the cat suddenly darted toward the room with the mirror, its tail flickering nervously. It stopped in the doorway, staring intently at the abandoned room.

Lila followed, as she entered the doorway, the black cat darted to the old mirror gazing at the reflective surface of the glass. She followed its intense gaze, feeling a sense of unease settle over her again.

"Do you see her too, little guy?" Lila whispered, half-expecting the cat to respond. Instead, it let out a low growl, ears flattening against its head. The tension in the air quickly thickened, and Lila's pulse became quickened.

"Alright, little guy," she murmured, "Let's figure this out together."

She grabbed her flashlight from the floor, exactly where she had dropped it earlier, and approached the antique mirror once more, but the black, tabby cat wouldn't let her get too close. It interposed itself between her and the faded glass of the mirror, its body nervous and tense. Lila knelt beside the black cat, curiosity piquing. "What is it, little fellow? What do you see, what do you know?"

Suddenly, the old mirror rippled again, and Lila felt a slight pull, as if something beyond the glass was calling for her. In that moment, the mere reflection in the glass shifted, and a scene unfolded, faintly... a vibrant garden filled with blooming flowers of various design, where Eleanor played happily with a black cat that looked strikingly similar to the one by Lila's side.

Then the vision turned dark. Shadows loomed heavily over the garden, creeping closer to Eleanor, who was smiling and laughing with her pet, blissfully unaware. The image of the black cat began to hiss as it arched its back with its hair standing straight up, desperately trying to protect Eleanor. Lila felt a tight knot form in her stomach, as she realized what she was actually witnessing... a mere memory of love and impending danger. With a small gasp, the vision in the glass shattered, and the black cat beside her leapt back, its green eyes wide with alarm, "What happened?" Lila asked out loud, almost in shout, her voice trembling, yet determined. "What happened to you both?"

The cat sat, its gaze intense as it continued to stare at the old mirror, as if urging Lila to piece together the fragmented memory. She thought back at all the articles she had read in the library, rumors of strange occurrences in the mere garden, pets disappearing, and faint whispers of estranged curses. "I need to locate this garden," Lila decided aloud, glancing back at the antique mirror, "Maybe it holds the key to Eleanor's past, and yours too." she stated as she looked down at the black cat.

The dark, tabby cat meowed softly now, as if in agreement, then darted out of the room. Lila sprang to the doorway, curiosity and great concern propelling her forward. She hastily followed the black cat through the dim hallways, her flashlight beam flickering across the dimly lit walls of the old house, illuminating faded portraits that seemed to watch her journey. Lila decided in her thoughts that she would remove these portraits first thing in the morning.

Lila and the mysterious black cat made their way to the back of the mansion, where a set of double doors led outside to the backyard. Lila pushed them open as the black car darted through, revealing a hidden garden overrun by ivy and wildflowers and tangled in disturbing vines. Lila quickly began sneezing but finally shook it off. Moonlight spilled over the haunting scene, creating an otherworldly glow.

"Wow," Lila breathed, taking in the mere beauty and chaos of the spacious garden. It felt untouched, as if time had forgotten it, but the faint echoes of faded laughter and whispers still lingered in the air. The tabby cat bounded ahead, weaving through the foliage intil it reached a large, ancient oak tree. It sat beneath the tree's gnarled branches, staring up as if waiting for something to happen.

"What is it, little guy?" Lila asked, her voice a mere whisper, as she knelt down beside the black cat. She slowly scanned the area with the beam of her flashlight, her instincts tingling with anticipation. Beneath the roots of the old oak tree, she noticed an irregularity, a small, weathered box partially buried in the earth. With determination, Lila began to dig with her free hand. The moist soil was damp and cool, and soon enough, her fingers wrapped around the box's edge. She pulled it free from the dampened dirt and brushed away the dirt, revealing intricate carvings of flowers and vines. It was beautiful and eerie all at the same time. This little box was very old, tht much she could tell.

The black cat meowed again, nudging Lila's hand with its head. With a mix of excitement and trepidation, she finally realized this cat was urging for her to open the antique box. Inside it lay a collection of small trinkets, a delicate, faded silver locket, a faded photograph of Eleanor with the black tabby cat, and a crumpled piece of old parchment paper. Lila quickly unfolded the fragile parchment paper, it was a letter, written in elegant cursive, filled with words of love and longing, though slightly faded, she could make out its words. The letter spoke of a secret meeting, a promise made beneath the oak tree, and a warning of dark forces that threatened to tear them apart.

"Eleanor," Lila exclaimed, her heart beginning to race, as she whispered the words, "This must be it! You were trying to protect something precious!"

As she read, the mere atmosphere around her shifted, and the shadows deepened. The black cat's growl resonated again, this time louder, more urgent. Lila looked around, feeling an unsettling presence stirring in the air. Suddenly, the ground beneath her trembled. Lila's heart raced harder as she realized that her and the black cat was not alone now. Shadows twisted and morphed, forming into menacing shapes that reached toward her and the tabby cat. "Run!" she shouted, scooping up the little antique box and sprinting back to the mansion, the black cat close behind her. The shadows urged after them, still swirling all around, a swirling mass of utter darkness determined to reclaim what had been unearthed.

Once inside, Lila slammed the double doors shut, pressing her back against them as she caught her breath. The black cat sat at her feet, wide-eyed and alert, its soft fur bristling.

"Not again," Lila whispered, clutching the box tightly, "What do those creepy shadows want?"

The air was heavy with spooky tension, but in that moment, Lila felt a flicker of determination inside her. She was part of this mysterious haunting now, and with this strange black cat by her feet, she would uncover the hidden truth, and help Eleanor find peace.

"What's next?" she asked, as she looked down at the black cat, who was looking up at her as if ready to guide her deeper into the mystery. Lila concluded within her thoughts that her and the black cat would face whatever was next, whatever lay ahead. No matter if the black, tabby cat was just merely a ghost cat...

Chapter 4

The Lady in White

The night wrapped around Lila like a cloak as she huddled in the drawing room, the mysterious box cradled in her lap. The flickering light bulbs seemed to cast eerie shadows that danced along the walls, mimicking the shapes of the estranged figures that still lingered in her thoughts. The black, tabby cat sat close at her feet, its green, emerald eyes glinting with an intelligence that sent a slight shiver down her spine.

"What now?" Lila whispered, glancing at the black cat, then turning her gaze to the antique box. The faded silver locket glinted enticingly, and the crumpled old letter held the secret promise of answers. She could feel the weight of Eleanor's unfinished story pressing upon her, urging her to dive deeper. She carefully opened the fragile locket, revealing a tiny photograph in black-and-white of Eleanor, her eyes seemingly bright with life. On the opposite side was a small lock of hair, brittle and delicate. Lila closed her brown eyes, imagining the warmth of the woman who once wore this locket, the mere laughter that had filled the air around her, but then she remembered the creepy shadows, the urgency in the faint voice of Eleanor.

"I promise, I will help you, Eleanor," Lila said softly to herself, holding the locket close, "But I need to know what exactly happened to you?"

Suddenly, the black cat meowed, and the air turned cold, and a gentle breeze swept through the room, extinguishing the lights to a dimmer glow. Slight darkness seemed to envelope Lila, but just as panic threatened to take hold, a soft glow illuminated the corner of the drawing room. Lila squinted, her heart pounding. From the shadows emerged a bright figure, clothed in a flowing white, lace gown that shimmered as if woven from the moonlight. Long dark hair cascaded down her back, and her face, though ethereal, bore an expression of sorrow tinged with faint hope.

"Eleanor?" Lila breathed, recognizing the glowing silhouette from the visions earlier tonight.

The glowing figure glided closer, the air around her pulsing with unseen energy, "I am not Eleanor," she said, her voice, faint, a melodic whisper that sent chills down Lila's spine. "I am the Lady in White, a mere guardian of lost souls."

"Guardian?" Lila echoed, confusion mingling with awe. "What exactly do you mean by 'guardian'?"

The Lady in White nodded solemnly, "I am bound to this place, this house, protecting those who cannot find their inner peace beyond death. Eleanor was my friend, and her sweet spirit is tethered to the sorrow of this mansion."

Lila's mind raced with questions, "Well, what happened to her? Why can't she just move on?"

The Lady in White's eyes glimmered with unshed tears, "Eleanor loved too deeply, but her heart was betrayed. The dark shadows you encountered are mere remnants of that betrayal, born from the cruel darkness that enveloped her mere fate."

As this ghostly figure spoke, Lila felt a surge of empathy. She understood now that Eleanor's past was not just a spooky story; it was a tapestry woven with love, loss, and unwilling, unfulfilled promises. "How can I help her?" Lila asked, desperation threading her words.

"Find the truth hidden within this house," the Lady in White replied, "The answers lie within the simple shadows, but be warned... they do not take kindly to those who seek to uncover their secrets."

'Then I will face them," Lila declared, bravely, her voice hardening, "I won't let Eleanor's story end in this eternal sorrow."

With a faint smile of acceptance, the Lady in White gestured toward the abandoned room where the mirror dwelt, "The reflection reveals what the heart cannot see. Seek its truth, and you will find the way to free her trapped spirit."

Before Lila could respond, the glowing Lady in White began to fade away, the bright glow of her presence dimming until only the shimmering essence remained, "Remember," this lady ghost whispered before she completely dissolved, "love is the key."

As the last trace of the Lady in White vanished, Lila felt a renewed sense of purpose. She turned back to the black tabby cat who still dwelt next to the armchair, motioning for it to follow her to the abandoned room where the antique mirror was located. As she looked at the old mirror, the flickering reflection seemed to beckon for her to step closer. The black cat brushed against her leg, its purr vibrating loudly with anticipation.

"Okay, let's do this," Lila said, taking a deep breath. She stepped forward, her fingertips grazing the cool surface of the vintage mirror. The glass rippled, and the familiar scenes began to swirl, revealing flashes of a past that was long ago buried.

This time, the ballroom appeared vividly, vibrant with much laughter and music, Guests twirled in elegant ballgowns and sharp, tailored suits, but Lila's focus was on Eleanor. She stood at the center, her fragile face radiant with joy, yet Lila sensed an undercurrent of tension in the air around Eleanor. A man entered the scene, his presence commanding and dark. The music shifted, and the faint laughter faded even more into hushed whispers. Lila's heart sank as she recognized the sinister energy surrounding him. He approached Eleanor, a charming, wicked smile masking a malicious intent.

"What is this? Who is that bad man?" Lila whispered, clutching the faded silver locket in her palm tightly, "No. don't trust him, Eleanor!"

Eleanor danced vibrantly with this estranged man, but Lila could see the unease in her fragile eyes. They exchanged words, their expressions growing serious. Lila tried to listen closer, trying to catch snippets of their faint conversation, but it was almost impossible to hear. The sounds of their voices seemed to grow louder, and Lila was able to catch a few of their words, "Your family stands in the way," the estranged man said, his voice smooth but laced with threat. "We could rule together, your fortunes, but you must let go of your past."

Eleanor's gaze darkened, and she pulled away from the man, "I will never forsake my family for mere power, sir."

The man's wicked smile faltered, revealing the darkness within him, "Then you will suffer the consequences."

Suddenly, the vision shifted violently, plunging Lila into chaos. The dark shadows emerged, surging forward, wrapping around Eleanor like tendrils of heavy smoke, pulling her into utter darkness. Lila screamed into the mirror, desperation rising as she watched Eleanor struggle against the force, while the black cat hissed and jumped around at Lila's feet.

"Help me!" Eleanor's voice echoed, blending with the whispers of the cruel past, "Find the truth!"

The scene shifted again, now showing the garden where Lila had discovered the vintage box. Eleanor sat beneath the ancient oak tree, the black, tabby cat at her feet. A moment of peace surrounded them both, but it was fleeting, the dark shadows creeping ever closer to them. Lila felt her heart start to race, "I can't let this happen again!" she turned her gaze to the black cat at her feet, who seemed to sense her urgency, "We need to find the source of these dark shadows... there must be something in that garden!"

The images in the old mirror faded away, as Lila, with a determined nod, and the black cat leading the way, darted through the mansion's hallways until they reached the garden once more. The night air crackled with unseen energy, and the dark shadows hovered at the edges, just watching, waiting.

"Stay close," Lila whispered to the black cat, as if she needed to protect it, as she approached the ancient oak tree again. The memories of such betrayal and cruel darkness swirled around in her mind, but she would not back down. She began to dig deeper as the flashlight lay on the moist ground next to her. She dug so deep that she hit the roots of the oak tree, beneath these roots, she unearthed more secrets that had long ago been buried. As she dug further, the ground trembled again, and the shadows stirred, rising ominously, "You should not be here!" a strange voice boomed, echoing like thunder.

Lila's breath quickened as the dark shadows formed into estranged, vivid figures, twisted and grotesque, "Leave now, or suffer the fierce consequences!"

"No!" Lila shouted in reply, clenching the locket in her hand tighter, "I won't be afraid! Eleanor deserves to be free, to find her peace!"

With renewed, determined courage, Lila continued to dig like she was going insane, her fingers scraping against something hard, she pulled it free with slight force, revealing a small, ornate box, similar to the one she had found earlier, yet slightly larger. This one, however, bore a darker, wicked aura, and Lila felt the shadows closing in around her. The black, tabby cat hissed, its fur standing on end as it leaped protectively in front of Lila, "Stay back!" she commanded, her voice steady, as if the ghost cat needed protection.

With shaking hands and faint sight through the smoky shadows that continued to swirl around her, Lila opened the old box, inside lay a small vial filled with a swirling, dark substance. As she held it up, the shadows writhed, their vivid forms and smoky allures distorting in fear of the vial. "This is it!" Lila realized, "This is what binds Eleanor, a mere potion laced with a curse!"

As the shadows lunged all around her, Lila threw the opened vial into the center of the garden, shattering it against the ground. Dark, smoky mist poured out, filling the air with an oppressive weight, but as it spread, it began to dissipate, the light of the full moon pushing back against the darkness.

"No!" the dark shadowy figures screeched, their mere forms twisting in agony, "You cannot..."

But it was too late. The darkness receded, and with it, the oppressive weight that had haunted the old mansion for so long. A soft light emerged from the ground, illuminating the area around the ancient oak tree.

"Eleanor!" Lila cried, feeling the warmth of the light wash over her. The air felt lighter, as if the garden had been cleansed of its sorrow. Eleanor had been released from the captive, vintage mirror, as she hovered in the mist of the garden. As the last remnants of the dark shadows and smoky haze vanished under the moonlight, the Lady in White reappeared, radiant and filled with joy. "You have done it, dear girl," she said, her voice a soothing balm. "You have freed Eleanor's trapped spirit from its chains."

Lila felt a swell of relief and joy as she turned to the black, tabby cat, who purred loudly beside her, "We did it together, little guy!"

In that moment, the garden slowly began to blossom with vibrant colors, the flowers swaying gently as if in gratitude. From the depths of the moonlight, Eleanor's spirit glowed, her presence warm and serene.

"Thank you," Eleanor whispered, her eyes glistening with sparkles of tears that radiated pure joy. "You have given me back my peace. Although, my life can never be returned to me, you have set my eternal spirit free."

As Eleanor stepped forward, the Lady in White extended her glowing hand, guiding Eleanor toward the ethereal light that shimmered in the center of the garden. Lila felt warm tears streaming down her cheeks, a bittersweet mix of sadness and great joy.

"Will I see you again? "Lila asked, her voice trembling.

Eleanor only smiled softly; the mere weight of her sorrow now lifted. The Lady in White spoke, "In every bloom of the garden, in every whisper of the wind, she can be with you. You have brought peace to her soul."

With that their spirits both began to fade into the light, a soft melody pf faint laughter echoing around Lila. The shadows that once held the mansion captive were now gone, replaced by a mere sense of hope and renewal. As the garden transformed into a sanctuary of beauty, Lila knew this was only the beginning. She had faced the darkness, and now the light of Eleanor's spirit would always guide her in whatever lay ahead. With the black, ghostly, tabby cat by her side, she stood proudly, ready to embrace the next chapter of her new life, filled with inner love, light, and satisfaction, along with the mere promise of a new beginning in this old mansion.

Chapter 5

The Victorian House

The morning sun spilled through the windows of the old Victorian mansion, illuminating the remnants of the night's hauntings. Lila stood in the garden, as she began to yawn, surrounded by vibrant flowers that seemed to bloom brighter under the early morning sun. The air seemed fragrant from the scent of all the flowers, and the weight of sorrow had finally lifted, replaced by an exhilarating sense of peace, yet, even in this newfound peace, Lila felt a lingering pull, a sense that her journey in this new home was far from over.

As she gazed at the majestic garden, the black cat curled at her feet, its green, emerald eyes glimmering with an understanding that transcended words, "What now, little guy?" Lila mused, glancing down at the tabby cat, "Where do we go from here?"

The cat's ears perked up, and it meowed softly, then gracefully trotted away from the garden, toward the old house, looking back as if urging her to follow. With a sense of purpose, Lila brushed the dirt from her jeans and followed the black cat into the old house. As they both entered the threshold of the mansion, leaving behind the echoes of Eleanor's past and embracing the promise of the unknown, Lila smiled. She went straight to her bedroom with the 'ghostly' cat at her side and went straight to bed...

As she wandered through the now-bright hallways that next afternoon, unpacking her boxes, Lila felt the old house was alive and energetic. The oppressive shadows now gone, faded, and the bright sunlight flooded every room, revealing the mere beauty hidden beneath all the layers of dust. As she unpacked and cleaned away some of the ancient dust, the black, ghostly cat still lingered with her. They both moved room to room, as Lila rearranged some of the old furniture, and covered the vintage mirror with a large, white sheet. She definitely did not want to ever look into that glass again. As she made her way further into the mansion, placing random decorations and such throughout, she noticed a strange shaped, wooden door that felt completely ominous. She noticed it was ajar, as if inviting her and the black cat inside. Curiosity piqued, Lila placed the box she was holding onto the wooden, hallway floor, and pushed the heavy door open to reveal a small, dust-covered library, its shelves lined with vintage, frail books and antique, yellowed pages. In the center stood an ornate Victorian table, its surface cluttered with strange trinkets and relics from a forgotten time. Among them, a small music box, old and fragile, caught her eye, its delicate craftsmanship very captivating.

As Lila approached the vintage table, the ghostly, black cat leapt gracefully onto a nearby wicker chair, watching intently. She picked up the delicate music box, its intricate designs etched into the wood. With a gentle twist of the small, skeleton key, it sprang to life, filling the room with a haunting, beautiful melody. The mere sound washed over her, evoking memories of dances long past, of laughter that echoed through the halls, as if she were there in the past itself. Suddenly, a chill filled the air, and the music faltered. Lila glanced around, her heart starting to race. Shadows flickered at the edges of the room, swirling like wisps of clouds, "What is happening now?" she whispered, gripping the music box tightly, as the black cat stared in amazement. Lila's mere thoughts swirled in her mind at the mere idea that a new spirit was trying to contact her...

The cloudy shadows coalesced into a lovely figure, a woman dressed in a flowing Victorian gown, her faint features soft yet tinged with melancholy. "You've awakened me," she said, her voice echoing like a distant memory. "I am Isadora, once the lady of this house."

The black cat jumped down from the chair, as it ran over to Lila, she took a step back, instinctively clutching the cat for reassurance, "Isadora? What do you want?"

"Not what I want," Isadora replied, her expression wistful, "But what I need. My spirit has been bound to this house since my untimely passing. The darkness you vanquished has only partially freed me. I seek the truth of my own demise."

Lila swallowed hard as her heart kept racing with a mix of fear and sympathy. "How can I help you, what must I do?"

Isadora gestured toward the library's shelves, "There are secrets hidden within these walls, mere remnants of a life once lived. The answers you seek to your unspoken questions lie in the pages of my past."

With fearful curiosity and determination, Lila moved toward the bookshelves, scanning the titles that lined the dusty books, as she sneezed, the black cat jumped from her arms returning to the wicker chair. She pulled one book from the shelf, 'Whispers of the Past: The Haunting Chronicles'. The spine was cracked as she gently opened it, and she felt the weight of ancient history pressing in. The frail pages told a story of the first family to live in this Victorian house many years ago, who actually had this mansion built, their rise to prominence, and the shadows that clung to their mere legacy. As Lila read, she discovered tales of unrequited love, betrayal, and an ill-fated romance between Isadora and a man named Victor, who had harbored very dark ambitions.

"Victor," Lila murmured, recalling the same man from Eleanor's vision in the mirror; the actual drawing of this man was in this book. "What exactly happened between you and Victor?" Lila asked as she turned to face Isadora, who was patiently waiting in the corner of the room.

The cloudy shadows seemed to shift, as if stirred by Lila's question. Isadora's eyes glistened with unshed tears, "Victor was a charming man, wealthy, but his heart was twisted by much greed. He sought power through manipulation, and I unwittingly became his first pawn in his endless game. When I finally agreed and married him, we had this Victorian house built, yet he became over-controlling and took matters into his own hands."

The fragile, old music box continued to play softly, and Lila felt the weight of Isadora's inner pain, "What did he do to you?"

"He unleashed darkness upon this very house, binding my spirit to its walls," Isadora said, her voice trembling, "In my final moments, I sought to protect my family that I loved, my mother, my father, and my brother, but Victor wanted our inheritance, and when I refused to allow him such, he became evil, his dark magic becoming evident. It costed me everything, including my life, yet I just couldn't allow him to corrupt my heart. All I had left was my music box, given to me by my mother. Victor knew it was my most prized possession, so, he cursed it from ever playing music again. You are the first one to get it to actually play, Lila."

Lila's heart ached for the poor woman standing before her, "How can I help break such a curse? Will it release you, so you can find peace?"

"Seek the truth of my final moments," Isadora urged. "There is a hidden room within this house, a place where Victor practiced his mere evilness, a place where he plotted my demise. It is the key to freeing my trapped spirit."

With a sense of urgency, Lila nodded. "Where exactly is this hidden room?"

Isadora's expression softened, and she pointed toward a dusty portrait hanging on the faded wall, "Behind that portrait lies the entrance, but be cautious... Victor's darkness lingers there still."

Lila swallowed hard, taking a deep breath, as she approached the creepy painting of what appeared to be Victor, a heavy frame adorned with intricate carvings. With another deep breath, she grasped the edge and pulled it aside. To her astonishment, a small door was revealed, its wood dark and very aged, as if it had not been opened for many centuries.

"Stay close." Lila whispered to the black cat that was not next to her feet, perching attentively. As she opened the door, Isadora's spirit lingered behind her, the creaking sound of the door echoing in the mere stillness of the dim library. Inside was a very old, narrow staircase with candle holders lining the path, the candles were frail yet still intact. This ancient staircase led down into utter darkness. Reaching into her jeans pocket, she pulled a cigarette lighter out, that she had found in one of her boxes while unpacking. On her journey down the creepy stairs, she lit every candle, illuminating a steady glow. Lila felt a cool shiver of apprehension but pressed forward. "We have to do this, little guy," she said in a whisper, determination steeling her resolve, as the black cat followed her.

The steps of the staircase were damp, cold against her bare feet, and the air grew heavier with each descent. At the bottom, she emerged into a dimly lit chamber, candles already burning all around it, its mere walls were lined with strange symbols and ominous smoky shadows that seemed to dance like phantoms. A large, ornate table sat at the center, covered with dusty, vintage scrolls and remnants of long-forgotten rituals.

"This must be it," Lila breathed, stepping cautiously into the chamber. The mere atmosphere was thick with tension and slight fear, and she could feel the remnants of Victor's malevolence pressing down upon her. As she approached the table, she spotted an ancient book lying open, its pages old, yellowed with age. She leaned closer trying to focus in the dimly lit chamber, deciphering the faded text: 'The Binding of the Shadows, A Dark Pact'. The mere title, the mere words inside spoke of sacrifices made to gain power, of darkness unleashed in exchange for wealth and control.

"Victor's journal," Lila realized, her heart racing again. This was the truth that Isadora sought.

Suddenly, the smoky shadows in the room writhed, coiling around Lila like serpents. "You should not be here!" a voice boomed, echoing with fury. The mere air crackled with dark energy, and Lila felt the temperature drop.

"Victor!" she shouted, her voice steady despite the fear coursing through her. "You won't keep Isadora's spirit bound any longer! I will free her from your dark magic, just as I did Eleanor's spirit!"

The dark shadows formed into a dark figure, a tall man with piercing eyes and a malevolent grin, "You are a foolish girl to think you can challenge me. I will not allow anyone else to escape my bindings."

As the tall figure, which was Victor, advanced, Lila reached for the fragile music box still clutched in her hand. She remembered the Lady in White's words... 'love was the key'. "Isadora!" Lila called out, feeling the warmth of the soothing music envelope her, "I need your strength!"

In that moment, the music filled the entire chamber, resonating with a powerful energy. The shadows recoiled, the air shimmering with light as Isadora's spirit fully appeared beside her, radiant and resolute.

"You will not bind her to this house, Victor!" Isadora declared, her voice a fierce echo in the chamber. Together, Lila and Isadora, stood against Victor's dark magic, the light of their combined spirits pushing back all the dark, smoky shadows.

"You think you can defeat me?" Victor sneered, but his bravery faltered as the light grew brighter from Isadora, "No! I will not be denied! You will not defeat me!"

Lila felt the power surging through her body from Isadora, igniting her courage, "Isadora, we must break the binding! Together!"

With a slight nod, Isadora raised her ghostly hands, and the music from the vintage, frail music box swelled in response. The smoky shadows began to dissolve, and Victor's tall figure twisted in agony. "You cannot do this to me!" he roared, but his voice trembled as the light consumed him.

Lila focused on the journal, reciting the words, loudly, she had read, "With love and truth, we break these chains, that bound Isadora to this dwelling! Let the shadows give her full release, and shall they return to such a void!"

As she spoke, shouted these words, the room erupted in a blinding flash of light. Victor's tall figure dissipated, swallowed by the radiance, and the shadows that had clung to the faded walls vanished, leaving only a soft glow behind. When the light dimmed again, the chamber felt much lighter, the oppressive weight gone. Isadora stood beside Lila, her expression one of profound gratitude and peace. The black cat resurfaced from behind the chairs in the corner, purring proudly as if it was truly alive.

"You have freed my spirit." Isadora whispered, tears seeming to form in her ghostly eyes, "Thank you, Lila, for your courage, and for the bravery that you showed when you freed my granddaughter, Eleanor... I must confess a truth to you now, my children were not Victor's, but his brother's, who was my only true love..."

Gasping, Lila felt a wave of warmth wash over her as she blushed at Isadora's last words, all she could say was, "You deserved to be free, to be at peace."

With that, Isadora stepped toward the bright light that appeared suddenly, her fragile form shimmering with much grace, "Remember, love is always the key that unlocks the darkest of hearts. You carry it deep within you, this mere love."

As Isadora vanished into the light, Lila felt a sense of closure for her, and a sense of closure for Eleanor. The darkness that had haunted the old mansion was now gone, or so it seemed, replaced by an overwhelming sense of hope and renewal. The tabby cat meowed softly, brushing against Lila's leg. She knelt down, feeling the warmth of the creature beside her, as she thought of how this mere cat was so warm to be deceased, "We did it," she said, her voice filled with amazement and slight wonder.

As Lila and the black cat left the dim chamber, the candles flickered and went out, she knew her journey within this old house was far from over, she could just sense it. The old mansion held more stories untold, more spirits longing for release, Lila could just feel it. But she also knew she was not completely alone now, with the ghostly, black, tabby cat by her side, she would face whatever came next. Lila decided to name this ghostly animal, calling him, Ghost. The cat meowed loudly purring, as to accept his new name. Together, her and Ghost, emerged into the frail light of the library, ready to explore the next chapter when it arises, the next adventure in the haunting yet beautiful world of the old Victorian house.

Chapter 6

The Red Eyes

The sun dipped below the horizon, over the next few days, casting long shadows across the old Victorian mansion. Lila stood in the library, as she cleaned and rearranged all the antique books, the remnants of Isadora's spirit seeming to still be lingering in the air, filling her with a sense of peace and accomplishment, but as the twilight deepened, an unsettling sensation crept into her bones, a feeling that something was not quite right.

The ghostly, black, tabby cat, that she named Ghost, who had been napping contentedly, suddenly perked up, his ears twitching as it scanned the room. Its body tensed, and it let out a low growl, the sound reverberating through the silence. Lila felt her heart start racing, "What is it, Ghost?" she asked aloud, her voice nervous.

Ghost bolted toward the small window; its eyes locked on something outside. Lila followed, peering through the glass of the small window, the last rays of sunlight illuminated the garden, but something shifted in the shadows. Two glowing red eyes pierced the dimness, watching her with an intensity that sent shivers down her spine.

"What on earth...?" Lila murmured, squinting to get a better look. The eyes were large, gleaming with an otherworldly redness, and they seemed to belong to a creature lurking just out of sight. As she stepped closer, the red eyes blinked slowly, then vanished, leaving the garden shrouded in the faint darkness. Lila's pulse quickened, "I need to see what that was, Ghost!"

With Ghost at her side, she opened the double doors, after venturing through the old mansion, and ventured out into the garden. The cool night air wrapped around her like a hazy fog, and the garden felt alive with whispers and rustling leaves, "Stay close, Ghost," she whispered to him, as if he was merely a living animal. Ghost could sense her unease, so, he stayed close like she said to do. They both moved cautiously through the garden, Lila's heart still racing, pounding as she scanned the shadows for any sign of the mysterious creature. The moon hung low, casting an eerie glow, illuminating the twisted branches and darkened paths.

"Maybe it was just our imaginations, Ghost," Lila said, reassuring herself, though she couldn't shake the feeling that something was watching. Just as she turned to head back to the old house, the red eyes appeared again, this time closer and much brighter, reflecting the mere moonlight like rubies.

"Show yourself!" Lila called out, her voice steady despite the slight fear creeping in. "What do you want? Why are you here?"

To her surprise, the red eyes vanished once more, and a soft rustling filled the air. Lila's instincts kicked in; she crouched low, with Ghost perched next to her, peering into the weeded darkness. Ghost stayed alert, ready to pounce if necessary. "Come on, I know you are there," she urged, hoping to provoke a response. Suddenly, the rustling grew louder, and from the shadows of the weeds emerged a sleek, shadowy figure, a large, white cat with striking red eyes that seemed to glow with an eerie light.

Lila's heart raced, "Another ghost cat?" she whispered, but there was something unsettling about this one. It moved with a predatory grace, red eyes that were locked onto to her with an intensity that sent chills down her spine.

Ghost hissed, fur bristling, as he positioned himself protectively in front of Lila. "Easy, Ghost," Lila whispered, feeling the tension rise, "Let's not escalate this."

The white cat tilted his head, watching her and Ghost intently. Lila could feel his intense gaze piercing through her, as if he were weighing her soul.

"What do you want? Why are you here?" she asked again, her voice trembling slightly at the white cat's red eyes.

Suddenly, the ghostly, white cat opened its mouth, revealing sharp teeth. "I am not your enemy," he said, his voice low and smooth, sending a ripple of disbelief through Lila, "I am a guardian of this realm, this house, a keeper of the hidden secrets within the mere shadows."

"Guardian?" Lila echoed, as she just realized that she was speaking with a ghost cat... trying to process the revelation, of this cat talking, actually talking. "But why the red eyes, and why are you even here? Do you have a name?"

"I am drawn to those who seek the truth", the white cat replied, its eyes narrowing, "But be warned, the path you tread is fraught with danger. There are those who wish to keep the past buried, and yes, I have a name..."

"Like Victor? Is he the danger?" Lila asked, interrupting, her mind swirling with questions. "Is he still out there, dwelling somewhere in this house?"

"Yes, he is," the white, guardian cat confirmed, flicking his tail. "Victor's darkness, his mere evil, still lingers within these walls of this house, and he will stop at nothing to reclaim his eternal power. You have successfully freed some of the spirits trapped by his evil, but there are others still bound to his will. The red eyes you see on my face are a mere warning symbol, Victor still watches, waiting for an opportunity to strike."

Lila felt a chill run down her spine, "What do we do about it?"

"You must uncover the remaining truth of Victor's past," the white cat urged. "There is another chamber within the mansion where his darkest secrets lie, only by confronting them can you truly banish him."

With this newfound knowledge, this new, arising sense of purpose, Lila nodded. "Lead the way."

The white cat turned, gliding through the garden with an elegance that belied its feral nature. Lila and Ghost followed closely, her heart pounding again with slight fear and much determination. They retraced their steps back to the old mansion, moving through the now-familiar hallways. They, all three, arrived at a mysterious door that Lila never noticed before, a hidden tapestry that depicted a grand mystery. The white, guardian cat paused, looking back at her with its piercing red eyes. "This is it. Inside lies the truth you seek."

Lila felt a mix of trepidation and excitement. "Are you coming with me?" she asked as she glanced down at the red-eyed cat.

The white cat shook his head. "I can only guide you to the mere threshold. The confrontation is yours to face."

With a deep breath, Lila nodded. "Well, let's get this over with, Ghost." she said, determined as she gestured for the black, tabby cat to lead the way into the chamber. Pushing open the door, the hinges creaked ominously as it revealed a dark, hidden chamber. Lila gripped her flashlight tightly. Inside, the air was thick with mere tension, and the walls were lined with more strange symbols and many ominous artifacts, trophies of Victor's dark dealings. As she stepped further inside, Lila felt the weight of dark history pressing down on her. In the center of the room stood another ornate mirror, similar to the one she had encountered before with Eleanor, but this one was slightly different, its surface shimmered with a darker energy, and the reflections were warped, revealing distorted images of past horrors. This mirror seemed larger than the one she had seen before.

"Stay alert," she whispered to Ghost, who faithfully remained close by her side. Lila approached the massive mirror, compelled to look at it deeper, what she saw in the glass made her gasp.

In the faded reflections, she witnessed a vision of Victor's past, a life steeped in much darkness and cruel ambition. Scenes unfolded before her... Victor charming Isadora, manipulating her mere trust, and finally, the moment of betrayal. Lila saw him casting dark spells, binding spirits to do his bidding, feeding on their utter despair. "Isadora!" Lila cried out, watching the pain unfold as Victor took her life by a knife to her throat, binding her spirit to this old house, but there was more... a flicker of another figure, a petite woman with strikingly similar features as Isadora, watching Victor from the shadows, her mere expression twisted with much jealousy and rage.

"Who is that?" Lila whispered aloud, wondering, "Why is she so angry?"

The white cat's voice echoed in her mind, although it was still patiently waiting behind the door's entrance to the chamber, "The petite woman is Lydia. Consumed by her jealousy, she had aided Victor in his dark ambitions, seeking to usurp Isadora's place."

Lila felt a slight surge of understanding as she heard the white cat's faint voice in her head, "Lydia was behind these bindings as well. She had betrayed Isadora also."

The reflections shifted again, revealing Lydia's desperate attempts to wrest control from Victor. She was as manipulative as he was, using her mere charm and cunning to secure her own power. Just then, a chilling laugh echoed through the damp chamber, resonating from the depths of the mirror. "You actually think you can uncover the truth? You are much too late, little girl!"

Lila's heart raced harder in her chest, as if it was going burst through her ribs, as she recognized the voice... it was Victor. The old mirror pulsed with dark energy, and smoky shadows twisted around her, drawing her closer. "You will never escape my grasp!"

"Not if I can help it!" Lila shouted, summoning up her courage. She remembered Isadora's words to her, about how love was the key, "I won't let you win!"

With newfound determination all of a sudden, Lila focused on the mirror as the shadows continued to swirl all around her, Ghost quickly made his exit, hiding behind an old, worn-out bookstand across the chamber. Lila began reciting the words she had read in the ancient book of the library, similar to what she had read aloud before. "With love and honesty, I break these chains! Let the dark shadows return to the unknown void!"

The air crackled with much energy as the ancient mirror trembled violently, the mere reflections distorting in chaos. Victor's form flickered within the faded glass of the mirror, rage radiating from him. "You think you can fully banish me forever? I will return!"

As the smoky shadows surged toward her, Lila stood her ground, pouring her heart into her words, "You have no power here! You will not take any more lives!"

The energy around her intensified, and the ancient mirror, suddenly, exploded in a blinding flash of bright light. The dark energy was pushed back, the evil shadows being pulled into oblivion, dissipating into the air like a hazy smoke. Lila shielded her eyes with her arms, hoping the shards of glass wouldn't cut her up, and when the light finally faded, she found herself standing there, alone, and quiet within the chamber. The old mirror was shattered, destroyed. Thankfully, the pieces of glass from the old mirror never harmed her.

In the quiet aftermath, Lila felt the oppressive weight of darkness lifted, as if a heavy curtain had been drawn back. Ghost quickly ran over to her, rubbing against her jeans, purring with much gratitude.

"Is it over?" Lila breathed, her heart still racing.

The white, red-eyed cat appeared behind her, its eyes gleaming brighter with much approval. "You have faced the mere darkness and uncovered the dark truth, Victor's hold on this place, this house, has weakened, but his mere evil spirit may still linger, just waiting for a chance to surface again."

"Then we will be ready, ready to defeat him again!" Lila shouted as she looked around the chamber, as if speaking directly to Victor. With a settled determination in her heart, she said, "I won't let that happen. Victor will not bind anyone in this house ever again!"

The white cat nodded in approval. "Your mere strength lies not only in your courage but also in the mere bonds you have forged. Seek the truth and you will continue to protect this realm, this mansion. Always remember, I am here to protect... and my name is Seth..." The white, red-eyed cat disappeared.

Lila nodded in appreciation as she left the damp, hidden chamber, she felt a renewed sense of purpose sweep through her, as her heart stopped racing, there was a slight calmness within her. The mere journey in this old Victorian house was still far from over, that she knew, but with Ghost at her side and the knowledge she had gained, she was ready to face whatever challenges might lay ahead. Together, her and Ghost, stepped back into the hallway of the mansion, closing the door tightly to the hidden chamber.

Chapter 7

The moon hung high in the night sky, illuminating the old, Victorian mansion with a silver glow. Lila stood at the threshold of the hidden chamber with the door tightly closed, her heart still calming down within her chest. She pondered on the confrontation with Victor and the shattered, old mirror that lay within the hidden chamber, completely destroyed. Its remains were simply a remnant, a testament, to the power of truth and courage, but she knew the mere darkness wasn't completely vanquished. It lingered in her instincts like a small, faint storm cloud, waiting for the chance to return.

Ghost brushed her leg, grounding her in the present moment, "We need to find the remaining spirits, Ghost, and put an end to this mess." Lila murmured, her resolve firm. "There are stories still untold, and we can't let their darkness remain, these innocent spirits have to be set free and find their peace."

The black, tabby cat, Ghost, still lingering at her leg, purring in agreement, merely nodded his head. At that moment, the white, red-eyed cat named Seth, appeared in front of her, making her and Ghost jump in fear.

'Don't just appeared suddenly like that!" Lila screeched as she recognized it was Seth. Ghost hissed loudly, as he ran past and headed downstairs.

Seth nodded apologetically, as he said, "More souls are lost, trapped by the shadows, bound to secrets long buried, only you can uncover their tales, only you can truly set them free, truly cleansing this place, this mansion."

"I know, Seth," Lila responded, as she rolled her eyes, taking a deep breath. Lila felt the weight of much responsibility settle on her shoulders. She recalled the whispers in the garden, the laughter that once filled the halls, and the memories that still echoed in the mere corners of this old mansion. It was time to bring those hidden stories to light.

"Where do we start, Seth?" she asked, as Ghost made his return, placing himself next to her feet.

"Just follow the echoes." Seth replied, as he gave a faint meow, "The mere spirits trapped here will reveal themselves now, to those who listen." With that, the white cat disappeared again.

Lila looked down at Ghost, then back to the hallways in front of her, that stretched before her like a small labyrinth of mere history. She had explored the many depths of this place, this old house, unearthing secrets of the past, hidden within these walls. Lila thought on the idea of how the locals in town would react to the actual truth about this old house, but she knew they would only believe her to be insane, she merely chuckled a small laugh at the thought.

After several days of peacefulness, Ghost and Lila continued to unpack her boxes and place everything in the right places through-out the house. As they ventured into the parlor, one afternoon, its once-grand furniture still draped in white, dusty sheets, Lila sneezed. Pulling one sheet away, more dust particles dancing in the dim light of the room, she felt a faint presence, a gentle breeze of coolness that seemed to carry faint whispers from another time. "Can you actually hear that, Ghost?" she whispered, as she looked in circles around the massive room.

With a soft meow, as if he was answering back in a whisper, Ghost stood at alert, ears perked. Lila closed her eyes as she sneezed once more, letting the murmurs wash over her. The voices were quite faint, but urgent, urging her to merely listen, to try and understand.

"Help us... remember..." one voice called out, echoing like a distant chime.

Lila opened her eyes, "Who's there? What exactly do you want?"

As if in response, the air shimmered, and a figure emerged, a young girl with flowing blonde hair and a tattered dress, her blue eyes wide with fear and longing, "I am Clara," she said, her soft voice echoing like a lullaby. "I was lost in the darkness, but now, I remember..."

Lila knelt down, her heart aching for the girl's plight, "Clara, what happened to you?"

Clara glanced around, her mere gaze filled with sorrow, "I was playing hide and seek with my mother when the dark shadows took me away. They dragged me down into the depths of the house, and I was trapped within the walls, forgotten."

"Not anymore, Clara." Lila promised, determination flooding her veins. "I will help you find your peace."

Ghost stepped forward, purring in sympathy for the little girl, as he rested next to Lila. Suddenly, the white cat, Seth surfaced just on the other side of Lila, stepping forward, its red eyes glowing brightly with a fierce intensity, "Clara, the truth is your ally. What all do you remember about your past, about the mere darkness?"

Clara's expression shifted, a flicker of recognition crossing her fragile face, "I saw... I saw Aunt Lydia. She was angry, desperate. She sought to steal my mother's light and keep it for herself."

"Lydia? Her aunt?" Lila echoed in a whisper, trying to piece together the past history that had been shrouded in the shadows. "Lydia was a part of this too?"

"Yes," Clara replied, her voice trembling. "She turned to the dark magic, seeking much revenge. The dark shadows were her allies, and she used them to bind us all here, along with Victor, she trapped us here in mere anger."

"Then we must confront her. Who is your mother, sweetie?" Lila declared, asking in curiosity, the fire of resolve igniting within her. "We need to find Lydia's unsettled spirit and help her move on."

The white cat, Seth made his disappearance, as Lila continued to gaze at Clara with heartfelt sympathy.

Not answering Lila's question, Clara slowly faded away, her mere presence leaving behind a shimmering light. Lila felt the slight weight of responsibility grow heavier upon her. The old mansion was steeped in layers of so much sorrow, and she had to uncover them all. Moving from room to room, Lila and Ghost, searching for any clues to where Lydia may be dwelling, where she may be haunting. In the library, they found another spirit, a young man, handsome with blonde hair and blue eyes, named Thomas, who had been a very loyal friend to Isadora. He recounted tales of much betrayal and sorrow, revealing how Lydia had manipulated all those around her, twisting love into mere darkness. Thomas confessed to being Isadora's lover, her one true love, and the actual father to her children.

"Lydia was not always cruel," Thomas said, his voice heavy with slight regret, "But such jealousy consumed her, and in her mere quest for power, she lost everything, including her family."

With each spirit they seemed to encounter, Lila and Ghost, she gathered more pieces of the story, each small tale echoing the pain of a past that refused to be forgotten completely, that wanted to be told, revealed. The weight of their sadness pressed down on her, but with each new revelation, she felt her own strength, determination grow. With the manly spirit of Thomas lingering behind her and Ghost, they ventured through the dimly lit mansion in search of Lydia's spirit.

Finally, she stood before a door at the end of a long hallway within the mansion, a door that seemed to hum with a dark energy. Ghost regarded Lila with a serious expression, "This is it, I can feel it," Lila whispered, as she nodded to Ghost. "I can feel that Lydia's spirit lingers here, bound by the mere darkness of her own making. Are you ready, Ghost?"

With regained courage and determination coursing through her, Lila said aloud, as she looked back at Thomas's spirit behind her, "We have to set her free."

With a faint nod from Thomas and Ghost, Lila slowly pushed the heavy door open. Inside was a small chamber room bathed in shadows, the air was thick with much sorrow, and at the center stood the mere spirit of a petite woman, Lydia. She was flickering like a candle in the wind, dressed in a black, lace, Victorian dress with a frail hat, her eyes glowing with much rage, much anger. "Why have you come?" Lydia hissed, her faint voice a mere mix of anguish and slight fury. "You dare to disturb my eternal rest, my damnation?"

"We are here to help you, Lydia. We want to set you free, help you find your peace." Lila softly replied, her voice steady despite the slight fear coursing through her. "You've been consumed by the darkness for so long, but it does not have to be that way any longer."

Lydia laughed bitterly painful screeches, the sound echoing off the dampened walls, "Peace?" There is no peace for me. I was utterly betrayed by my brother, left behind while Isadora thrived. I sought power to reclaim what was rightfully mine, what I had lost, and now I am bound to this place, this house that I had desperately wanted.

Victor was my cruelest brother, I thought he actually cared for me, that he would leave me with great riches. He promised me the entire world, until he met her... Isadora, and had her children, one being Clara, her oldest child, along with our younger brother Thomas, who I see is with you now. Victor turned on me, binding me here in this house, after I helped him bind all the others in his dark desires for control. He lied to me! He gave me nothing, only an eternity of damnation within these walls! Thomas deserted me as well, when he fell madly in love with Isadora and had all those little girls, three lovely girls, who stole all his affections from me!"

Lila slowly, cautiously stepped forward, her heart aching, breaking for the petite woman before her, "You are not alone anymore, Lydia. You don't have to remain in your pain. We have heard your story; we have heard your sorrows. We want to help you; we want to set you free and help you move on."

Lila recalled the words she was told from Isadora and the Lady in White, 'Love is the Key'...

"Love? Help?" Lydia scoffed, but Lila could see the faint flicker of sadness, doubt in her eyes, "Why would they want to help me? I have done too many terrible things to all of them."

"Because they understand your pain now, Lydia." Lila said, her voice softening even more with much sympathy. "They know the darkness of Victor only consumed you by his false promises, hie mere lies, and they know that you are good deep inside yourself, beyond your bitterness and pain. We all, Thomas, Clara, and I, want to set you free from such darkness, give you your eternal peace."

As Lydia's expression faltered, Lila felt the energy shift within the room. "You can find redemption, just embrace the light instead of the darkness, break free from the shadows that bind you."

For a brief moment, silence enveloped the chamber. The faint dark shadows around Lydia began to slowly retreat, swirling like a fine mist, revealing glimpses of the saddened woman, giving a faint allure of the peaceful lady she once was, full of life and hope. "I'm not sure I can," Lydia whispered, her voice full of regret, "I've lost so much now."

"Just let the past go, embrace your eternity in the light," Lila urged, easing closer, "Release all the sadness, all the anger and pain. Allow the light to guide you now."

With a hesitant breath, Lydia closed her eyes, the mere shadows around her shivered and dissolved, a soft light began to glow within her, pushing against any darkness. Lila reached out her trembling, yet calm hand, feeling a deep inner connection forming, a thread of mere empathy that transcended any struggles.

"You can do this, Lydia," Lila whispered, "You are more than your regretful choices, your cruel darkness. You can choose to embrace the light, the mere love you once felt."

Lydia slowly opened her fragile eyes, and for the first time in many years, they were not filled with such rage, such anger and pain, but with a flicker of renewed hope, a peace. "Is it too late?"

"No." Lila replied as warm tears formed in the corners of her eyes. "It's never too late to love again."

With a surge of sweet energy, Lydia released a heart-wrenching cry as the faint shadows that lingered fully vanished, leaving behind a radiant light. The chamber room pulsed with energy, and as the darkness retreated, the glowing spirits of Clara and Thomas appeared next to her, their peaceful faces now filled with love and much forgiveness.

"Together," Clara said, her fragile voice like a gentle breeze.

"Let' go." Thomas added, extending his hand to Lydia and Clara.

As they, all three, joined hands, a brilliant light enveloped them, lifting their, now, peaceful spirits from the depths of much despair.

With one final glance, Lydia smiled, a smile that held the weight of a thousand regrets but also the promise of such redemption. Love really had been the key. With a blinding flash of a bright light, the chamber room was filled with gracious, pleasing energy, and the three spirits began to fade slowly, leaving behind a sense of closure, a sense of peace, that resonated throughout the entire mansion.

Lila stood in the center of the vast chamber room, warm tears slowly streaming down her face, as she felt the warmth of their release. "It's done," she whispered, the mere weight of any darkness lifting from her shoulders. "They are all free now."

The tabby, black cat, Ghost hovered at her feet, happily, purring loudly, as if to celebrate. The white cat with red eyes, Seth, appeared, stepping forward, his red eyes now shining with much pride. "You have done it. You have faced the darkness and brought forth the light. You have uncovered the truth, the untold stories, tales, and set all the trapped spirits free. Thank you."

"No, thank you, Seth," Lila said, her heart swelling with much gratitude. "I have done my best, and now, they are all at peace."

"Indeed." Seth graciously replied, "But you have showed great courage and strength, along with much compassion. The mansion will be at rest now, and all the spirits shall watch over you, wherever they have gone in the great beyond." With that, Seth disappeared.

As Lila and Ghost left the chamber room, Lila felt a sense of calmness wash over her. She would always remember, honor the memories of all these spirits that she helped release in this old Victorian house, who had come before her, sharing their faint stories of their past. The old mansion was no longer a place of fear, it had become a bright sanctuary of much hope and renewal. With Ghost, her ghostly cat, still haunting her, at her side and the mere lessons of love, she had learned etched within her heart, Lila would continue into her new beginning in this old house, she would embrace whatever life has to offer her within this realm of untold tales that may surface within these walls.

And so, the darkness of the past for those mere spirits faded into nothing more than a memory, replaced by the light of a new beginning, forever guiding Lila's path forward. She had overcome the shadows of the untold tales, a simple collection of fearful happenings within a family that was twisted by one man's greed... May they all, now, rest in peace.

The End.

Darkness... Untold Tales
(Collection of Fearful Happenings)
By: Anna Elizabeth

Darkness... Untold Tales (Collection of Fearful Happenings)

www.ingramcontent.com/pod-product-compliance
Lightning Source LLC
Chambersburg PA
CBHW072128150726

47999CB00005B/2185